How To Make Money Online In 2020

The Ultimate Guide To Passive Income On Autopilot

Gregory McCallister

TABLE OF CONTENTS

© Copyright 2019 by Gregory McCallister 4

INTRODUCTION 6

CHAPTER ONE 8

AFFILIATE MARKETING 9

Commission Autopilot.................................14

CHAPTER TWO 19

EMAIL MARKETING 20

The Ultimate Opt-in Email Marketing Tool 24

3 Quick and 'Dirty' Steps to Your Own Huge Payday..28

Email Marketing - How to Make Your Profits on Autopilot...30

CHAPTER THREE 33

WEB ADVERTISING 34

Various Forms of Web Advertising.............36
CHAPTER FOUR..42
AUTOPILOT LIST BUILDING....................43
3 Benefits of Building a List on Autopilot..45
How to Make Money - List Building...........49
CHAPTER FIVE 54
FOREX AUTOPILOT SYSTEM 55
Why Do We Have to Use Forex Autopilot? 58
Three Rules to Avoid Forex Autopilot Scams
....73
CHAPTER SIX...77
MONETIZE YOUR BLOG 78
CHAPTER SEVEN...86
AUTOPILOT MONEY MAKING WEBSITES
....87
Websites That Makes You Money...............89
CHAPTER EIGHT...92
AUTOPILOT ARTICLE MARKETING.......93
CONCLUSION 103

© Copyright 2019 by Gregory McCallister

All rights reserved.

This document is geared towards providing exact and reliable information with regards to the topic and issue covered. The publication is sold with the idea that the publisher is not required to render accounting, officially permitted, or otherwise, qualified services. If advice is necessary, legal or professional, a practiced individual in the profession should be ordered.

From a Declaration of Principles which was accepted and approved equally by a Committee of the American Bar Association and a Committee of Publishers and Associations.

In no way is it legal to reproduce, duplicate, or transmit any part of this document in either electronic means or in printed format. Recording of this publication is strictly prohibited and any storage of this document is not allowed unless with written permission from the publisher. All rights reserved.

The information provided herein is stated to be truthful and consistent, in that any liability, in terms of inattention or otherwise, by any usage or abuse of any policies, processes, or directions contained within is the solitary and utter responsibility of the recipient reader. Under no circumstances will any legal responsibility or blame be held against the publisher for any reparation, damages, or monetary loss due to the information herein, either directly or indirectly.

Respective authors own all copyrights not held by the publisher.

The information herein is offered for informational purposes solely, and is universal as so. The presentation of the information is without contract or any type of guarantee assurance.

The trademarks that are used are without any consent, and the publication of the trademark is without permission or backing by the trademark owner. All trademarks and brands within this book are for clarifying purposes only and are the owned by the owners themselves, not affiliated with this document.

INTRODUCTION

These days it seems like everyone is interested in learning about ways that they can make a little extra cash without having to go out and look for a second full-time job. Hard-working families are struggling to make ends meet while maintaining a healthy family environment, and the last thing they need is for one or both parents to be gone from the home more hours out of the day. With the success of so many internet businesses all over the news, many people are becoming interested in how to make money online.

The only problem with starting to research how to make money online is that everyone has an advertisement or commercial about how they have the secret plan that will make you rich in a week. After a while, weeding through all of the bogus scams and worthless schemes is enough to make any reasonable person throw up their hands in disgust. If you've found yourself in this position, you may be wondering, "Are there any legitimate ways to make money online that don't require a big scary investment on my part?" And the answer is yes.

The first thing to do when learning how to make money online is to look for a plan or guidelines that don't ask for a huge investment up front. Be wary of so-called online business gurus that claim to have all the secret strategies for making money online, but require that you pay them hundreds of dollars in order to learn even just one strategy. Just like with so many other things in life, honesty is the best policy. If the inventor of one of these strategies is really confident that his or her plan will be successful for everyone, then they won't be afraid to share a few of the tips they gathered, because they will be so sure that you will see the worth of the plan and buy it anyway.

If you are serious about learning how to make money online, don't be afraid, you are on the right track reading this amazing eBook! In this eBook, I will teach you a series of ways of making money online via autopilot. However, you must realize that as with anything in life, you will have to put in some work, at least in the beginning, before your business will really make money, but the payoffs will be very worth it. Keep reading if you want to know how to make money online in autopilot mode.

CHAPTER ONE

AFFILIATE MARKETING

Autopilot Profits is a series of videos and an e-book that shows you how to make money in affiliate marketing by automated online delivery of products and services. Autopilot profits also offer a free exploration software download which can give you a turnkey plug-and-play style business which lets you begin making money immediately. The videos and books show you how to make money from hundreds of thousands of people who look to the internet for products and information.

When you look at affiliate marketing and business, there are four areas that you need to conquer in order to be successful:

Finding a focused niche market.

A product or service in that niche that people are looking to buy.

A marketing strategy to present your product or service to prospective buyers.

Away to automate the development and sales process as much as possible.

Autopilot Profits presents a step by step system to make money in the shortest possible time. The system gives you only the important information that you need to start making money right away and eliminates the filler seen in so many other programs.

If you've read other Internet marketing guides that have given you a plethora of strategies and vague promises, Autopilot Profits will bring it all into focus and deliver information that is concrete and ready to use. It will jump over all of the mistakes that most new businesses make on the Internet and leave you with just those essential facts that make successful businesses on the web.

It's easier than you may think to put the four steps listed above into action. You need to find and focus on a niche where there is an unmet demand. This video series and e-book will show you how to do exactly that. Picking the right niche market is essential to internet marketing success.

When you do manage to find a niche market, you will need to find out what you can sell there based on market surveys. If you can't find an appropriate product, then you won't be able to make profits and sell services or products. If you are going to be putting in a lot of effort and expecting large returns out of it, you need to have a solid product, which everyone wants to buy, so do your market research accordingly.

Autopilot Profits gives you the marketing techniques to present this product or service to your target market in a way that will make them want to visit your website, ready to buy.

Autopilot Profits will teach you how to automate most of these tasks, letting you have a business that essentially runs itself. You can do this with minimal startup costs (usually less than $100) and start making money right away, with little intervention needed on your part. Autopilot Profits can benefit everyone, from affiliate marketing newcomers to seasoned internet marketing veterans. This is a program that really works - try out this e-book and video series today.

More and more people are realizing that the living they are making barely allows them to survive with dignity and are looking for ways to supplement their income. Most people have now been reduced to a life of paycheck to paycheck. However, Affiliate Marketing has given new hope to people, so that they can build up businesses that will offer long term profits and allow them to lead a better quality life, with a better work-life balance. The Autopilots profits system allows you to make money online by helping you to generate ideas that return good profits.

Make Money Online With Autopilot Profits

You can make a steady profit by just sparing a few minutes a day through the Autopilots Profits System. This system allows you to generate a lot of traffic to your website and therefore ensure that you get a lot of sales and that too within a few hours of setting up your business.

One of the Fastest and Simplest way to start your Autopilot Online Business

This system shows you how to find a hungry crowd. In the hungry crowd we mean people who are looking for an answer to a problem and then creating a product or service, to answer that problem or question. Your crowd should be passionate about this specific topic and want to learn more about. When you combine that with a specific need, you have created a person who will buy your product if it meets that need. The niche product can be about anything, from an answer to a specific problem or simple information about a subject that a person is passionate about.

This is what niche marketing is all about. One of the best ways to make money online is by filling the needs of a niche market; especially for internet marketing newcomers, it is best to avoid casting too wide of a net.

Niche marketing is where you find a small, tight-knit potentially profitable market segment that you can design products and services for. When you find this niche, you're going to want to build loyalty, and in that way, you'll be able to attain and maintain a profitable volume of sales for your product. When you hit this tipping point in terms of becoming an authority in a niche, you will build a loyal following who will probably buy from you again and again. This is the secret of niche marketing.

How do you go about identifying a niche audience to market your services to?

Autopilot Profits System shows how to tap into these niche markets and demonstrates how to find these potentially profitable niche markets. It also shows you how to identify larger niche markets that will be willing to buy a wider range of projects.

Autopilot Profits System provides you with a comprehensive, step by step system which is easy to follow and lets you start turning a profit almost immediately. What makes Autopilot Profits a truly one of a kind system is that it gives you only what you need to be successful in affiliate marketing or any other method to make money at home. Newcomers and pros alike can learn what they need to quickly turn a profit from the Autopilot Profits system.

Commission Autopilot

Commission Autopilot is extremely useful desktop software for automatic content creation as well as distribution for huge amounts of traffic, leads, and sales. You can use this program to make yourself viral all across the World Wide

Web and thus, earn huge amounts of money with affiliate marketing. The main aim behind using commission autopilot training and program is to place your website, blogs or affiliate links on top of the Google Search Engine rankings and obtain the highest possible page rank backlinks that point back to the offers of your choice.

By using this training and program, you would easily be able to gain the number 1 position on the search engine of your choice, whether Google, Bing or Yahoo. Not only this, but you will also be able to enjoy free traffic targeted directly towards your website. The best part about using this software is that you can earn profits with just an affiliate link. You do not even need to build up a website, sell a product or even buy hosting.

The Commission Autopilot Suite comprises of three different software:

Commission Activator

Commission Multiplier

This 2-in-1 suite helps its users to do the following tasks:

Generate traffic automatically

Create automatic backlinks

Carry out affiliate marketing strategies automatically with just a few clicks.

How Does It Work?

To use this program, all you need to do is open up the program and type in your targeted keyword. The program will automatically find the content matching your keyword. After this, you can use this software to convert that content to PDFs and embed them with your affiliate links. Finally, you can use the same program to submit your documents to various reputed document sharing sites.

In this way, you will be able to obtain top search rankings on all search engines like Google, Bing, and yahoo and generate huge amounts for traffic for your website, blogs or affiliate offers.

Who Should Use Commission Autopilot?

I highly recommend the use of Commission Autopilot for all kinds of marketers, especially:

Those who do not wish to spend too much money on advertising. With the help of this program, you will be able to promote all your affiliate links, without spending any money, to the targeted prospects.

Those who are not fond of building backlinks. With this software, you will get authority backlinks for free by just a single click of the mouse.

Those who are unable to generate traffic to their website/blog. Since you get free traffic from more than 18 reputable sites along with traffic from various search engines, you will be able to divert traffic towards your affiliate links without much effort.

Those who do not have much time to dedicate to the task of affiliate marketing. By using this software, you can easily promote numerous affiliate links, create high authority backlinks as well as generate huge amounts of search engine traffic with just a few clicks and without the need to devote too much time or effort to the task.

Without so many benefits, you can imagine the sheer number of visitors you can divert towards your affiliate links. Thus, the power of Commission Autopilot is evident, completely justifying the fact that it reached the top 5 listings on ClickBank within just a few days of its launch. Thus, the product is a must-have to all online marketers.

CHAPTER TWO

EMAIL MARKETING

This chapter is going to give you a secret that is so simple and easy to implement that you will kick yourself that you have not used it before. This secret strategy is different because you will learn how to make money from people who unsubscribe from your list. Obviously it is better to have someone stay on your list than to unsubscribe but if they are going to unsubscribe then why not make money from them since you will most likely never have contact with them again.

Few people are using this tactic even though it is so easy. As a matter of fact, very few so-called experts are using it. Who knows why what matters is that you are going to see how easy it really is.

The best part about this method is that it will not cost a penny to put into place and it takes anywhere from one to ten minutes to set up. The strategy is quite simple. Autoresponders typically send someone to a default page when they unsubscribe - usually a page that has info about the autoresponder and some type of message that says something like, "sorry to see you go".

If you are using opt-in email marketing then you have to have an autoresponder, there is no way around it. Most marketers do not realize that all of the good autoresponders allow you to can put in a custom URL to send the subscriber to when they unsubscribe. And this is where the secret lies. All you have to do is put a use a URL that is either an affiliate link for a product in your niche or use a URL that goes to a page that has AdSense ads above the fold of the page.

If you really want to see long-lasting results choose a product that pays monthly affiliate commissions. Obviously you are not going to get hundreds of people per day seeing this be every single person who unsubscribes from your list will see the offer or your page with the AdSense ads which will result in profits that you would not have made otherwise.

If you are going to have unsubscribed, and you definitely are, there is no way around it, you might as well make money off of them. You just got a free lesson in one of the easiest ways to make money online. What could be easier than making money on autopilot from people who unsubscribe from your list? If you are not doing this then you are leaving easy money on the table.

In order to send emails out to people on autopilot, you will need an autoresponder account with a reliable company such as Aweber or Get-Response. Once you have your account set up then you can start to add emails (or letters) that will go on schedule. When someone signs up to your list they will receive these emails on autopilot - without you doing anything.

Make sure that you include valuable content in your emails so that you are seen as someone who knows the niche topic. You need to build trust and respect with your subscribers. Every now and then you will send out an email that is promoting a product relevant to your subscribers. This might be your own product or it might be one that you know is good and you having an affiliate link for.

This is the link that you would include in your promotional email. Since you have worked on developing trust and respect, your subscribers are likely to click on your link to the sales page.

The sales page does its job of selling and if they purchase you makes money. More money if it is your own product of course! (If you create your own product then you needs to have this done beforehand to that your system can run on autopilot).

Traffic

Since this email campaign is already set up and ready to go all you have to do is get lots of traffic to your squeeze page for people to sign up to your list.

Your squeeze page will have an offer on it that people can receive for free if they sign up to your list. Therefore this offer needs to be valuable to your target market. Since we are talking about passive income, this traffic needs to be generated automatically - in other words without you being there!

Using content to drive traffic is a great way to generate traffic automatically. Your content is permanently out there for people to read or watch if it is a video and your squeeze page and email campaign is all set up and ready to work for you when people sign up to your list.

Getting the Online Results You Deserve

If you're not seeing the results you want with your online efforts then it might be down to what you're actually selling. I have discovered that when you create your own information products you are far more successful but you need to keep the momentum going and get products out quickly.

The Ultimate Opt-in Email Marketing Tool

Permission marketing has become one of the most effective strategies for marketing and selling virtually anything online. Many of the top online marketers rely solely on opt-in email marketing for growing their businesses and they focus all their efforts on building a database of qualified leads.

Permission marketing is based on a fundamental principle in selling, which is the simple fact that the majority of people will not buy something upon 'first contact'. This comes down to trust and online many people are reluctant to buy something from someone they don't know and trust. Opt-in email marketing is all about establishing relationships and building trust with potential customers.

If someone enters your website you have the opportunity to make them an offer. If they decline the offer and leave, then you've probably lost them forever. If you offer them something useful (that they need and are looking for) in exchange for their personal details you get to keep this potential customer forever. One of the most powerful opt-in email marketing tools is the power of building a relationship. Just like in 'real-life' relationships need to be built, cared for and nurtured to deliver. The same is true for building relationships online.

Sophisticated marketers online spend their time and effort on building relationships and they are constantly designing new ways of growing their opt-in email list. In many ways, this is a real challenge online. With a highly targeted and responsive email list, you can quite literally 'print' money because every email promotion you send out will return as money in your pocket. One of the most effective email marketing tools that are still extremely underused is that of co-registration.

With co-registration, you can put your list building efforts on autopilot and you can quite quickly build a rather big opt-in email list that is highly targeted and potentially very responsive. With 'traditional strategies you can easily spend weeks putting together an opt-in email campaign that yields little to no results. The reason why co-registration is one of the ultimate opt-in email marketing tools is that it's so efficient. You can buy highly targeted leads for as little as $0.30 per lead. The ability to make multiple offers to that lead, in the long run, is potentially worth ten to a hundred times your initial investment.

The prevailing trend of setting up a squeeze page with a free offer and driving traffic to the squeeze page via pay per click is fast busy losing its effectiveness. With so many free offers floating around it is becoming harder to get people to opt-in to your list. With co-registration, you bypass a lot of the problems involved in building an opt-in email list to market to. Co-registration is quick and you can rapidly build a huge list. It requires very little work from your side and the leads you capture tends to be of high quality - providing that you use a good co-registration service.

If you are serious about growing your online business then using co-registration as an opt-in email marketing tool can prove to be a very valuable investment. A highly responsive opt-in email list is one of the most valuable assets in online business and with co-registration you can rapidly grow your income and your business. If you are looking for a fast and cost-effective opt-in email marketing tool be sure to check out co-registration. If you consider the fact that a co-registration campaign will cost as much as a pay per click campaign, it's well worth a try and you only pay for the leads that actually opt-in to your offer and not just for clicks.

Co-registration does take a bit of trial and error to get right, but you can do some cheap testing and once you get it right you can scale your campaign and let it run on autopilot. Be warned though: don't jump in and try to get 100 000 leads on day one. Start small and keep tweaking it until you are happy with the results before you scale it up. Make sure you use a reliable co-registration service with a proven track record and not just some spamming service. Once you get the hang of co-registration you will see that it is one of the most effective opt-in email marketing tools out there - and the best part is that it is highly underused by the majority of marketers.

3 Quick and 'Dirty' Steps to Your Own Huge Payday

Here are the 3 quick and 'dirty' steps to having your own huge payday from email marketing (imagine sending out an email at 7 pm, and waking up the next day to a whole flood of orders! Do you want to achieve that? Then read on...):

1. Create a Free Product

You'd want to create a free product that you would actually sell if you could! The quality of the product must be that good if you want to build trust with your subscribers. The best kind of free product to create is an eBook or free report, which can be written in a day or outsourced to a ghostwriter.

2. Create a Squeeze Page

A squeeze page has one simple aim: to gather subscribers. It is usually short, with a benefit-driven headline, bullets emphasizing the plus points of opting in and the opt-in form generated from the autoresponder service such as Aweber or Gets Response. My advice is to study other squeeze pages in your market and see how they design their squeeze pages.

3. Send Huge Traffic to Your Squeeze Page

Now that you have your free product and squeeze page, you're pretty much all set to go. Here's how to send huge traffic to your squeeze page to start getting laser-targeted subscribers: pay per click marketing (really effective!), article marketing (good for long-term traffic), forum marketing (slow but steady) and co-registrations (huge list building on autopilot!).

Email Marketing - How to Make Your Profits on Autopilot

E-mail marketing is a very challenging task if you don't have the proper tool to get things done. You might be spending a lot of time answering e-mails hoping that this person will eventually purchase the product that you are selling. If you've been through a lot of affiliate marketing, an e-mail campaign is one of the things that you should consider but it will take your time if you don't have the right tools.

One of the known tools for a good campaign is automatic responder email marketing. Without this, you'll have a hard time sorting out every e-mail that you receive. For example, if someone opts in to subscribe to your newsletter, you may need to add him to your address book and look for the e-mail address when it's time to send the newsletter. Another scenario is that someone adds their email address to your website to request more information. You don't know what time they will enter their e-mail so you might want to be online for 24 hours.

Both of these scenarios are time-consuming and the returns are not good if you are still in your email marketing program. But if you have automatic responder email marketing, all you need to do is create the newsletter and send the e-mail through the autoresponder. The e-mail of your clients will be stored for updates since they have opted to receive your newsletter. If you have an automatic responder email, the client who is interested in your service will immediately receive free information about your service.

There are basically two kinds of autoresponders. One of them is quite difficult and will require more than simple technical skills. It's called the server-side type of autoresponder wherein the server is installed with an autoresponder. It works for big internet companies but for small businesses, there's not the server in the first place so it doesn't matter. However, the next type of autoresponder is perfect for anyone who is starting a small e-mail marketing campaign. Called an outsourced ASP model, you get an autoresponder company to take care of your mailing list. Everything could be done online. You'll be informed if there's a new e-mail interested in your newsletter or if someone unsubscribed to your newsletter.

When you have automatic responder email marketing, you don't have to be online to answer each of the e-mail coming in. The autoresponder will save you time, effort and ultimately money as you use your e-mail as a strong advertising campaign.

CHAPTER THREE

WEB ADVERTISING

Web advertising refers to some sort of promotion that utilizes the Internet to reach out to a wider audience. A lot of people so much into the Web these days that purchasing items and paying bills are even done in online transactions. Some good examples of advertising on the Web include rich media ads, banner ads, search engine results Web pages, social network advertising, online classified advertising, interstitial advertisements, e-mail marketing, and advertising networks. Most Web advertisements are catered by an ad server.

With regards to effective web advertising, there isn't any shortage of ways to get it done. Advertisers may use free options, for instance article marketing and social bookmark submitting, or they can opt for paid for advertising, for example, Pay-Per-Click (PPC) ads or paid link programs. Furthermore, there are link farms, blog and website networks, press announcements, forum marketing, and classifieds, just to name a few other available choices. When choosing the most effective web advertising for your business, it is important to consider the fact that many methods have, as of late, become useless to get a good search engine rank. For instance, big engines like Google are now filtering out link farms (pages that contain only links) since they're not considered useful content for searchers.

Similarly, networks of high PR sites and blogs that advertisers use for the sole reason for gaining backlinks are in danger of being discovered and turn off by Google, rendering links from sites useless and diminishing the effective web advertising that business owners worked so hard to attain.

Successful online advertising only happens when you use methods, which are okay using the search engines, so it's better to avoid black hat techniques such as these. In the end, there is still an array of white hat techniques that will produce effective web advertising for your business, for example, PPC, forum marketing, and countless other search engines - friendly methods. With that said, you need to remember that no single advertising method will be matched for every single type of business owner. It is important that an advertiser does their research and chooses the very best online advertising method or program that matches both their industry model and personal preference.

For example, if one does not like to write, then article promotion might not prove to be the most effective internet advertising method for that individual. Similarly, business owners with a lower budget may not be in a position to afford PPC costs (especially in competitive markets), which means paid ads will not be a resource of effective web advertising for that person. However, with so many possibilities, nobody must have a hard time getting a method of effective web advertising that works on their behalf!

Various Forms of Web Advertising

There are various methods and techniques of web advertising:

Pay per click

This is the latest web advertising technique. This is a performance-based type of advertising method and hence is preferred by most of the companies as well as advertisers. When a user clicks on the pay per click ad, he automatically gets routed or directed to the official web page or the official web site of the company or the advertiser. These pay per click ads need to be attractive and creative and should be able to catch the users' eye. The company pays the publisher or on the web site on which the ad is posted depending on the number of clicks that the ad got in the stipulated time period. The cost of the single click is decided by keeping the following factors in mind:

The popularity of the website on which the ad is going to be displayed.

The popularity and efficiency and usage of the search engine on which the web site is listed.

The search engine ranking of the web site and its ROI ratings

The number of popular and most searched keywords used in the ad.

According to the cost of the single click the final amount is calculated. The company or the advertiser needs to pay the money for the number of clicks that have taken place and need not pay any monthly fixed charges.

Permanent ads

Permanent ads are the traditional and primitive way of web advertising. Here the advertiser or the company needs to pay a fixed monthly charge to the publisher or the website as per the terms and conditions. The cost of the ad is more if the size of the ad is larger. Here the size of an ad is measured according to the number of pixels that are used by the ad. The cost of a single-pixel is decided by keeping in mind the following factors:

The daily traffic of the web site and daily visits

The user base of the web site and the content that is displayed or provided on the web site

The popularity of the search engine on which the web site is listed as well as the search engine ranking of the web site.

E-mail marketing is also a good way of web site advertising but is used only by a few people because it is not cost-effective and also does not give good results.

How to Make Money Using Web Advertising

Making money online has become feasible and increasingly popular in recent years. A lot of people are generating online income through the use of Web advertising. Gone are the days where people are spending much money on newspaper, radio and magazine advertisements, though some are still into it. Delivering marketing messages on the Web is so far the fastest and cheapest means of promoting products or services and increasing sales. Here are some ideas that can help you make money online through Internet advertising.

Have Your Own Website or Blog

If you want to make money on the Web, one easy way is getting advertising through a website or blog. You can monetize your blog by inserting advertising services into it like Google AdSense and other alternatives. Just make sure your website or blog contains interesting content or pages that readers will keep visiting.

Implement a Number of Website Advertising Tactics

If you want to drive traffic to your website to promote a service or product, you can use different website advertising tactics to maximize your income streams. Choose from pay per click (PPC) or affiliate marketing programs to even atypical tools that work efficiently than others. For some small business firms, improving online visibility is probably one of the obstacles they are trying to address. Nevertheless, Internet advertising can take much of the tension and help facilitate a steady income source.

Use Affiliate Marketing or Become an Affiliate

Whether you are someone who wants to make money online by promoting your products or endorsing other people's product, internet advertising is a good method that will allow you to do just that. Affiliate marketing is a kind of online advertising that is being used by many successful entrepreneurs for so long. The concept is straightforward. You hire affiliates who refer your products or services to you. Your website will drive more traffic this way and the affiliate marketer gets paid for every sale made because of his referral. So, it is a win-win situation for both parties. You can either sell a market or refer products to others to make money online.

Most Web enterprises were able to manage good savings on Web advertising as well as sales conversions by means of affiliate promotion. Just remember to use proper keywords when using Internet advertising to boost your sales, increase your earnings and make so much money online. You may put out some money in online advertising depending on the kind of advertising tools you will be using but once you have done it correctly, you will surely find that it is well worth trying.

CHAPTER FOUR

AUTOPILOT LIST BUILDING

The internet is full of websites and this chapter will give you the list building secrets you need to know but most of these "secrets" are useless, many relate to specific lines of business only and only the remaining few may be of some use to you. To get you started, here are some simple list building secrets - you can go on to more advanced techniques as you become more adept at the process. Begin by forgetting everything you have ever heard about the importance of building huge lists - there is nothing to be gained by having a list of 10,000 email addresses if 9,900 of them will never buy from you. A list of 200 potential customers is worth much more than an unfocussed list of thousands of names and for this reason, it is usually not worthwhile buying lists - they have no aim or focus and you do not know how valid the email addresses are.

Use a squeeze page with a free download to get email addresses - those who download something related to what you are selling are people who are interested in what you have to offer. Once you have a small list, ensure that the content you send them is of the highest quality and is sent regularly (that is the only way to keep their interest) - you need to continually remind those on your list that you exist and the material you send them must provide proof of your seriousness and the quality of what you are offering them. Once you have established a relationship with those on your list, you can start asking them for references - many will not respond but those who do will be the ones who see value in what you are offering and would like to give the benefit of that value to their friends - their recommendation will mean that half your selling is already done before you even send them your first mail. And do not stop with email addresses - discretely ask for more information to build up customer profiles, but ensure that you are not seen as being nosy as this could lead to your motives being questioned. You can do this by conducting surveys and opinion polls - but be careful never to seem to be nosy or intrusive as that will put people off.

Check out what your competitors are doing by joining their mailing lists under a different email address - it's a great way to learn their list building secrets. But keep mind that the most important of all list building secrets is not to worry about the size of your list but about how effective it is in getting your business.

3 Benefits of Building a List on Autopilot

Do you want to know how you can make list building really work for you? Since the online business industry is starting to become more and more competitive over the years, you need to make use of techniques that will ensure your popularity in your chosen field. Here are 3 benefits that you can expect to reap just by putting your list building functions on autopilot.

1. It gives you access to a much wider market

The great thing about doing business on the internet is that unlike traditional shops and stores, the internet never closes. This is probably why building a list on autopilot is not only possible, but it's also the logical step since it makes it a lot easier for you to become much more accessible to a wider market. Why settle within your local market when you can easily attract an international following?

2. Gives you time to focus on tasks that matter

If you're currently working in a one-person operation, you'll have more time to focus on more important business processes once you put list building on autopilot mode. Now, you won't have to manage your list on your own or spend hours looking for leads for your business. Just make use of a reliable list building program and let it work for you even while you sleep.

3. Saves you time and money since you get it all in one nifty package

And since there are currently different programs that you can easily have access to on the internet, you can choose one that has a number of features that you'll be able to put to good use. Look for a complete package that is guaranteed to save you time and money.

A Covert List Building Tactic for Getting Over 10 Leads a Day on Autopilot

Here is a list-building tactic to get over 10 leads per day on autopilot really fast: Classified ads. OK, they are not truly autopilot, in the sense that at the start of every day, you have to post your ad to classified ads sites. It only takes about 30 minutes to do it, and then you'll have 10+ leads into your autoresponder by the next day. Do this for a year, and that's 3000+ leads you wouldn't otherwise have!

Here's how to implement the classified ads strategy to growing your list:

Step One - Have a list of classified ads sites

Here is what my list looks like - Craigslist, MySpace Classifieds, Yahoo Classifieds, USFreeAds, Oodle and AdPost. These are the 6 sites I post to every day. You can make your own list too or just use these proven, high trafficked sites.

Step Two - Create a killer copy for your ads

Write about 3 to 5 ads for your lead generation offer and send your visitors to your opt-in page where you get subscribers. The reason why you need 3 to 5 ads is that you are going to test these ads over a period of a few weeks. Keep the ads that perform, and drop those that do not. Then create new ads to test against your well-performing ads. Keep on doing this to increase your response rates!

Step Three - Post your ads

At the beginning of your day or whenever you find about 30 minutes per day, post to the 6 sites I have listed above or to your own list of your websites and then sit back and watch your autoresponder generate leads!

How to Make Money - List Building

Discovering how to make money online comes down to learning how to build an interesting email list. Online entrepreneurs need to understand from the start that it is vital to have a group of contacts who are amenable to their marketing campaign. Possessing such a contact list will allow you to build your business as you build your list. Think about it for a moment. Having an email list means that you always have an audience ready to listen to what you have to offer. Such a list is a major asset for any Internet marketer, and should not be overlooked by any means. In fact, you must determine how to build a list of your own.

Hence, to consistently expand your business revenue over time, it is vital that you constantly add new subscribers to your opt-in email list. This is the lifeline of your online business. The individuals who reside on this list are the individuals who have essentially told you that they are interested in considering what you may want to sell to them in the future, so long as what you have to sell is of value to them. Having an email list gives you the ability to obtain the maximum time value from your customers, and also gives you the opportunity to turn a visitor into a future buyer.

So many new online entrepreneurs are on a quest to determine how to make money as quickly as possible with a short-term vision. This is why the failure rate is so high in online business. Rather, there must be a long-term vision supported by long-term goals. The fact of the matter is that it is much easier to build a receptive email marketing list than you probably think. To make sure that you get off on the right foot, we are going to discuss some of the most effective list building methods.

One of my favorite methods is a free giveaway. After all, who doesn't like getting something for free? What you offer your visitors can be as simple as a free eBook, software, or newsletter subscription. Just realize that in each instance, they have to give you their email address in order to receive what you are giving to them. The only thing that I must caution you about, is offering something which is of low value. For instance, so many products today have free giveaway rights. Essentially what this means is that you can purchase a product, along with the right to give it away for free to those who opt into your list. The problem with this is that many of your visitors will have already been offered this product on numerous occasions. How do you think this makes you look? Not very good. I always am for offering an eBook that you have written. The software can be ancillary to the main attraction, which is the eBook.

Another way to get things going is with article marketing. The nice thing about article marketing is that it gives you the ability to make yourself known to a large volume of people very quickly. Most article directories, to which you will send your articles, offer a resource box within which you can add a link to your website. Readers who like what you are saying will click on the link back to your website looking for more information. Of course, you will make it clearly evident that these readers can subscribe to your RSS Feed and receive articles directly to their email accounts every time you make a new post on your website. Guess what? You now have the email address. Feed the subscriber with a combination of valuable information, and offers which you think will be of interest to your niche market.

The unfortunate thing is that so many people do a great job of building their list, but then manage to mismanage the list. It is of the utmost importance that you first build a relationship with your subscribers prior to attempting to promote offers to them. The way in which you build a relationship is by giving them value. Yes, I understand that the whole reason that you took the steps to learn how to build an email opt-in list is to determine how to make money. However, your describers do not care about what you want. Rather, they need to see what is in it for them; otherwise, they will opt-out of your list. Therefore, it is important to first gain the subscriber's trust by becoming a resource to them. Shortly thereafter, you can suggest certain offers to them which you believe will be of interest. Keep in mind that people trust the endorsements of those who they know.

The good news is that if it is your goal to make a consistent income on the Internet with very little effort, then you must put a huge effort into building your email opt-in list from the beginning. Just remember that you must have a long-term vision to accomplish such a goal, and act consistently over time. Once you have your list, you will have determined how to make money.

CHAPTER FIVE

FOREX AUTOPILOT SYSTEM

Forex Autopilot system? What is this forex trading system? Where do you use it and why do you have to use it in forex trading? This automated forex trading system will help you automate your trading profits; I know you already heard about many successful forex traders who had been making a lot of money from forex trading with the use of an autopilot forex system. If you really want to be successful in the forex market you should at least learn the basics of forex.

Forex Market really involves a lot of risks. And risking your hard-earned money is so difficult to handle especially if you are in need of money. Many people don't want to take the risk and this is the very reason why many forex traders failed to make money from the forex market. But with the help of some technology we can now trade without having to risk, without having to worry and without exerting a lot of effort. Many people are searching for ways to make their trading more profitable without having to do some things that many expert traders had been experienced. They just wanted to make and earn money in the most possible and quickest time. And forex autopilot system can be used in achieving your goals.

Now, what makes the forex autopilot system different from the many forex trading software that has been spreading online? There are two popular systems that have been widely searched and used by many trading experts. One is the forex signals creator and the other one is the robotic forex trading system. The first one gives trader signals that are really helpful to their trading and the other one is an automated forex system that has been responsible for making trading so easy and profitable.

A lot of people are wishing for one of a kind forex trading system. They are wishing that they can to establish their own wealth online. With the use of the forex autopilot system, many people will surely make money! There are no software and system like this. Now here is the five reasons why many forex traders used this automated forex system:

Ease of use - Forex Autopilot System doesn't require any trading knowledge; you don't have to be a mathematician to start making money with it.

Fully automated - Now with the use of the forex autopilot system you can now enjoy life without having to worry so much about your hard-earned money place on trading the forex. You can make sure that you can make money even when you are asleep.

Flexibility - Forex Autopilot system works in any meta trader platform and works in any country. You can make profits even when you are not at home. As long as there is an internet connection, you really don't have to worry.

Zero investment cost - Forex Autopilot System will provide you an initial $100 for free to test their system on a demo account. Then if you already know the system flow then you can start with your real account and start reaping unlimited profits.

It is not an expensive trading system. Come to think of it, if you will join a trading seminar how much will it cost you? How long will you go to start making profits from it? But with the forex autopilot system you can start making money instantly.

Why Do We Have to Use Forex Autopilot?

There are lots of attempts to create a software or system that will help a trader to minimize risk and maximize their profits. All of this system has been promising a lot to the new and expert traders alike. The truth of the matter is quite simple however if you want a solution, all you need is a system that can identify and predict trends accurately and act upon them with precise timing.

This is the core of successful currency trading and it is based on what is known as the Fibonacci formula. With the onset of the computer age and sophisticated trading software, novice traders can drastically shorten the time it takes to profit from FOREX trading. One great way to do this is by using a forex autopilot system or forex robot. It is a completely automated currency trading system that identifies trends in the market and makes trades for you automatically.

The better FOREX trading robots will be able to maximize profits for you by picking entry/exit points based on sophisticated algorithms. Some come complete with money management tools that will compound your account automatically for you while minimizing risk.

If you plan to invest your money through the FOREX autopilot system, you need to do some searching. Some automated system charges you around $65 per month to use their program. Other than that, a minimum investment is required to participate in a forex trading robot. However, the forex trading system can reduce risk and improve overall system performance. Before you try on anything or decide to purchase a forex autopilot system you should consider the following:

You have to be sure that there is a free trial. Most of the forex autopilot system is offering free 8 weeks trial for you to see if the forex robot you purchased really works.

See if you can start with their demo account. This is really good especially if you are just new in the forex trading arena. Having a demo account allows you to trade even without investing any money. In this way, you will see the performance of the system without risking any of your hard-earned money.

Be sure that they are offering training, video and helpful information on forex trading. Most of the traders failed because they don't even know what they are doing. To be able to ensure profits, you must first start educating yourself. In this way, you will know the pros and cons of your action.

Make sure that the system that you have worked in any trading platform. The trading platform is very important in the forex market. It has a big contribution to the failure of a trader, the same thing with the forex signal.

Take note if the system has its money-back guarantee!

Maybe, you can have a better understanding of forex autopilot now. I hope that you can be successful in the near future. Deciding to choose from the different robot systems is very difficult but if you will going to use the simple step I was mentioned above, I know you will find the system that fits your trading needs.

Forex AutoPilot System vs. Forex Miracle

Forex AutoPilot System and Forex Miracle are 2 of the leading currency trading systems available. There has been much debate recently about which system suits which trader. In this sub-chapter, I will strip them back and reveal their strengths and weaknesses, and also unravel some myths that seem to be circulating about them.

Forex Robot or Forex System

Ideally, it depends on your level of experience in fx trading and what you want to achieve which will determine whether you choose Forex AutoPilot System or Forex Miracle. Forex AutoPilot is what is known as a forex robot - or automated currency trading system. Essentially you load it up with a bunch of presets - the defaults are 'meant' to be the most profitable, and then you let it do its thing. Forex Miracle, on the other hand, is a completely mechanical fx trading system. The creators of the forex miracle, Mark Kaplan and Kevin Hansen have literally devised there most effective trading strategies and documented them in the product. All you need to do is manually trade and follow the included instructions step-by-step.

Forex AutoPilot Strengths

FAPS allows anyone with a minimal trading system to begin trading immediately. While some knowledge of forex is advisable you do not need to watch the system like a hawk. Complete automation means you have more time to do other things.

Forex AutoPilot System Weaknesses

There has been quite a bit of bad press written about FAPS and in a sense, I can understand why. The product does not have that detailed instructions nor educational material for newbie traders. Furthermore, the settings do need to be experimented with - specifically the stop-loss setting which is crucial when you are trading with a robot.

Forex Miracle Strengths

Forex Miracle as mentioned is a purely mechanical system - literally step-by-step formula to trading successfully in certain conditions - which are relatively easy to find in the marketplace. I think the major plus of Forex Miracle is that you do not need a large amount of upfront capital to get results - in fact, the system was designed with this in mind. It also comes with very clear definitions of currency trading and how to trade effectively in today's economic environment.

Forex Miracle Weaknesses

I thought the presentation of the Forex Miracle EBook was a little cheap - but I guess you are paying for the quality of the information, not the presentation. Another negative is that you will need to invest time to firstly find and duplicate the settings and conditions then execute your trades with success. With an accuracy rate of over 90%, I guess it's probably worth the extra effort.

Forex Autopilot System and Forex Miracle are both worth considering if you are looking for a trading system that can leverage both accuracy and time for profit. I believe Forex Miracle is best suited to newbie traders who are always looking to invest as little capital as possible. Forex AutoPilot System, on the other hand, requires experimentation, decent capital, and experience to get maximum results.

Forex Autopilot vs. Forex Autopilot System

Forex Autopilot and Forex autopilot system are two phrases that has been playing an important role in Forex trading. Why do many Forex trader searches this kind of tools. Forex Autopilot and Forex autopilot system are both automated Forex trading system. They help even a beginner to make huge profits to the largest market we have today. They also help those people who have little knowledge about Forex trading. Many traders thought that they are exactly the same. Little did they know that they are different from many aspects? So, let's make the story short, how can you distinguish a Forex autopilot to a Forex robot.

The first one is designed by Marcus Leary, a mathematician who turbo charged his trading profits and brought the entire industry crashing to his knees. The system run on autopilot meaning you don't have to spend a lot of time checking your trade and profits. You just have to wait for your money to grow. It is a trading system that will show you the exact knowledge and training that will allow you to side step your competitor and super charge your income in to six figures. This system is a fully profitable business model in place guaranteed to make money. This system involves three simple and easy steps.

Download the trading system in to your hard disk.

Install and configure. Open a real demo account with our broker.

Run the advisors to your account and watch your business grow.

Meanwhile, the 2nd one is also known as the automatic money making trading robot and PAFS. It has been designed by Mark Copeland, a senior quantitative analyst in Goldman Sachs. He uses his 8 years' experience as an opportunity to research at the huge complicated system that the Forex expert uses to make killer trades for million dollars. He claimed that Forex robot is not just autopilot trading system but also a profitable system that let you possibly earns thousands of dollars a day. Forex autopilot system doesn't require any Forex trading experience and a fully automated black box software. Forex Robot is the only system with low risk and high gains up to thousand a day. It is a system that works in any country. It was just a system that you have to install and run. Forex Autopilot System will tell you exactly what to do and when to trade. The system will come along with a guide who instructs you step-by-step how to setup the system and use the system to trade. It will take you about 15 minutes to read the guide and 5 minutes or so to complete the setup and run the system. All the steps involve no cost. In Forex Autopilot system, the advisers given by the system has been explained. Your success with this system depends on your capital.

Forex Autopilot System Robot - Your Tool for Making Millions in Forex Trading

The Forex Autopilot System Robot can help you make millions in Forex trading. Until only a few years ago, the possibility of a forex trader becoming successful in placing winning trades in the forex market was only available to the few who were fortunate enough to acquire the right education to master the forex market. In the past, all those who tried to trade currencies on their own did not know that they were being scalped by smart people using a forex autopilot system robot. You now have the opportunity to make millions in forex trading with the right tool in your hands.

We all know that currency trading is characterized by complicated technical analysis. The variables facing anyone trading currencies are many. Our minds cannot keep pace with the speed of today's cutting edge forex trading software. Today, primarily due to changes in technology, the risk has been greatly reduced and the opportunity to make millions has been made available to virtually everyone who decides to invest in a forex autopilot system robot.

The forex autopilot system robot is not a human being with emotions and greed. Your emotions do not influence the operation of the software. Most times, your well-articulated forex trading strategies will fail you. At times too, a good forex trader may deviate from a great strategy after the latest new item.

The forex autopilot system eliminates the entire emotional trauma one faces in forex trading. It forces you to stay focus on your key strategy. There are stories of traders that would have lost so much but for their forex autopilot system, they were prevented from nose-diving wrongly into the market. We all know that any strategy is only as good as the individual's ability to execute the strategy and to identify the best opportunity to execute the strategy. Your forex autopilot system robot will help you take good care of your discipline and speed of calculation and execution.

The forex autopilot system is completely automated, powerful and effective forex software that will help you make killer trades in the forex market. The system will enable you earn thousands of dollars each day. Many traders are already using the forex autopilot system to automate their trading profits. Why not you?

The system will give you the financial freedom you have been dreaming of for years. You will no longer work long hours in a stressful working environment. All you require is to turn on your PC and watch the trades automatically executed and your millions will pour in on autopilot. The forex autopilot system robot is the right tool to make millions quickly in the forex market. In no time, you will be saying goodbye to the stress of your present work environment.

Frequently Asked Questions about the Forex Autopilot System

If you have done some research, you probably know a thing or two about the Forex Autopilot System and what it can do for you. However, when I first discovered this system I had a lot of questions even after some time using it. Therefore, I thought I would contribute by providing answers to common questions about this automated forex software.

What is it?

The Forex Autopilot System is basically a script designed to work within a metatrader4 platform, which is a popular suite designed specifically for forex trading.

How does it work?

The Forex Autopilot System works by installing it within your metatrader4 platform and from there, it will act as an expert advisor, analyzing trends and spotting opportunities for profitable trades.

What will it do for me?

The Forex Autopilot System is a software designed to work automatically, meaning that it places trades all by itself without any human intervention.

Do I need to have knowledge of the forex market or previous experience as a trader?

No, precisely, since you will not have to do anything but install and configure the Forex

Autopilot System, it is not necessary for you to have previous experience as a trader. In fact, I would say this is the best tool for the newbie trader.

How much money do I need to start trading with the Forex Autopilot System?

You can start with any amount of money you feel comfortable with. The minimum amount will depend mostly on the broker, but I would recommend you start at least with $500 and small lot sizes. Of course, always start with a demo account until you have familiarized yourself with the system.

What is the lot size?

The lot size is basically the value you assign to the pip (points of variation within the forex market). With an initial investment of $500, I would recommend starting with lots between 0.01 and 0.05 ($0.10 to $0.50 per pip). Indeed, although the makers of the Forex Autopilot System advise you to set the lot size at 0.1 ($1 per pip), I personally think that this value can be a bit risky if you have less than $1,000 in your account.

How do I know what is the right lot size for my investments?

There are different approaches to this issue depending on your risk tolerance, and many experts say you should not risk more than 3% of your account balance in a single trade. I personally like to use a margin of at least 1,000 times the value I set for the pip. This means that if I invest $1,000, I would not set the lot size within the Forex Autopilot System above the 0.1 value ($1 per pip).

How profitable is this software?

It is very profitable. Indeed, the Forex Autopilot System is very accurate, not meaning that it is perfect, but meaning that it is very consistent, so you will be getting a lot more winning trades than losing ones, which is what ultimately matters when it comes to steadily grow your account.

Do they really give your money back if you decide to return it?

Yes, the money-back guarantee offered on the Forex Autopilot System is legitimate, and they will issue a refund usually within 2 business days after you request it with no questions asked.

Do they have support?

Yes, they have a responsive customer service department in place to assist users with any issues regarding the operation of the Forex Autopilot System.

Three Rules to Avoid Forex Autopilot Scams

Forex autopilot systems are controversial. I guess that a smart forex trader who encounters forex autopilot trading software or any other kind of trading robot always asks the same question: Is this forex autopilot a scam? Well, in most cases forex autopilot software is indeed scams. They promise the moon but fail to deliver. Be aware of those.

However, it is just logical that there are SOME forex autopilot systems that do work. For example, it is well known that major investment banks do some forex speculation on a regular basis and it will be quite sure to assume that they are doing well. Have you ever thought who places the trades for those big institutes? True, they do have teams of professional's traders who analyze the economic news and get the "big picture". But as the forex market is open 24 hours a day, 5 days a week and the number of trades executed per day is huge, be sure that investment banks have automated trading systems that execute the trades. With a good build in money management and risk management rules; these industrial automated forex systems make a fortune for the big dogs in the long run. These automated money making software is among the best-kept secrets of the industry.

In the last few years, forex trading evolves and becomes available to private home-based traders. Soon enough, "home use" forex autopilot systems began to pop-up. As mentioned above, most of these systems worth nothing. But if you have a 9 to 5 jobs, using forex autopilot is probably the only way for you to start generating residual passive income from forex trading. So here are 3 rules you should follow in order to avoid forex autopilot scams:

Rule One: Look for a Money-Back Guarantee:

Never buy forex autopilot unless the merchant offers free risk money-back guarantee. Sellers who developed good systems have trust in their product and will not hesitate to promise you a full refund in case you are not satisfied. You should check very carefully the terms of the guarantee. Do not be lazy. Read the "small letters". Also, look for guarantees of at least 45 days, which is enough time to test the system with your demo account.

Rule Two: Check the vendor's Customer Support:

Do it before you buy. Serious vendors keep a customer support team that should be available during working hours on-line and via the phone. Simply contact the support team a few times prior to the purchase and ask questions such as: How will you refund me if I decide that the system is not for me? Has the system been tested prior to launching and for how long? What is the system's maximum drawdown? And so on. The answers you get (or not...) will help you to make a decision with confidence.

Rule Three: After you buy - demo trade your autopilot system:

Do not risk real money before you get to know your forex autopilot system. You WILL make technical mistakes and you do not want to pay real money for these mistakes. Take the time and master the software. Customize it to your own needs and trading style. If it works for you then fine - you have an additional income generator that might be your primary source of income in the future. If it does not work - ask for your money back before the guarantee expires.

CHAPTER SIX

MONETIZE YOUR BLOG

Starting your first blog is very exciting, I remember when I started my first one many years ago and although I didn't know much about websites and getting traffic I learned very quickly and it became a success. The biggest problem that most people have when starting their first blog is they don't have a person there telling them what they need to do and how to do it. For lots of first timers it is all a learning process but I want to help you get further ahead using my 5 tips to starting your first blog.

Adds Content - No matter if your blog is mostly pages or posts you need content to keep it going. Nobody likes to go to a site that has not been updated in weeks or even months. Here is what I do, one day I will write a post and another day I will write a page. Doing this will make your site bigger and it will help you rank better in the search engines.

Ping Sites - The greatest thing about having a blog is that you have the ping function included in it. What most people don't know is that a blog can easily get hundreds of visitors from other sites just by pinging them when you have a new post. The blog and ping method is very easy to set up and runs on autopilot once it is.

Create Backlinks - This should not be a surprise to you if you know anything about websites. The formula to get traffic to your site is - More backlinks = more traffic. When it comes to getting backlinks there are a few great places to get them, forums, other blogs, blog commenting, blog directories, and article directories such as ezinearticles.com

Interact - When I say interact I don't mean in person, I mean in the blogging world. The best thing to do is to start a conversation on another blog using the comment section and also keep it going back on your blog. Many people do this method and it seems to work very well. Remember, content is everything so if you have a post with hundreds of comments then it only helps your site.

Monetize - Do you want to make money with your blog? Most people want to make money with their blog and in order to do that; you need to monetize it (money-making options). The best ways to monetize your blog is to include Google Adsense, clickbank, amazon, and even sell links.

Monetization Techniques

Using blogs to make money was not a very popular method until four or five years ago when the number of blogs started to rise exponentially. A blog, in short, is a website where one has the freedom to share everything that comes to his mind. The word blog itself derives from the web and log. As of now, there are pretty much two types of blogs - personal blogs, which are to inform family members or friends about various events and activities. The second type of blogs is the ones we are going to concentrate on with this article - the business blogs. They are solely used to earn their author money. So many people are jumping into blogging since it is a source of the so-called residual income. This means that after a certain period of hard work and efforts, the blog will continue to produce money on autopilot.

Talking about making money through blogging is one thing and actually earning something is a whole lot different. There are various approaches and monetization models. Some of them can be quite effective, while others might turn out to produce close to nothing. This depends on a lot of factors, so trying as much as you can on your own is the only way to see what works for you the best. With the next few paragraphs, I would like to introduce you to 3 monetization techniques, which in my opinion are the best available out there.

Affiliate Marketing

Affiliate marketing is without a doubt one of the best possible ways to monetize a website. The method involves selecting a specific product, which is relevant to your blog's content and promoting it by adding reviews about it and lending links where appropriate. The product can be pretty much everything, but if you're offering information on marketing subjects, I would advise you to try your luck with e-books. Those sell quite well, as they are affordable and provide unique and in most cases useful information. So each time when someone decides to buy the product, you earn a commission (in most cases 50-70% of the product's actual price). The best place for beginning affiliate marketers is ClickBank.

Google AdSense

Google AdSense is one of the widest used monetization programs and there are not many who haven't heard at least once something about it. The concept is quite simple - using a number of various algorithms, AdSense places relevant ads on your site's sidebar. When someone cares to click on an ad you earn. Sometimes you may get as much as one dollar, while other times as low as one cent. This depends on a lot of factors, such as your site popularity, the time you're using AdSense, the site's topic and the advertisements themselves. There's also the option to earn from impressions - again the payment rates can vary and you get paid per 1000 impressions.

Selling Ad Space

Although that one can prove very beneficial, it is geared towards the more established websites. If you are getting a decent amount of readers, the chances are that there will be companies who'll offer you a monthly fee in order to place their websites on your main page. The bigger part of blogs I have come up charge around 15-20$ a month. You decide how much ads to put - the more you add, the higher the revenue you'll earn, but keep in mind that visitors would prefer a cleaner look and if the whole sidebar is full of ads, you might get readers scared away.

Sell Products from Your Blog

The truth of the matter is this: Most blogs don't make ANY money. Nothing. Zilch, zero, Nathan. If you are someone who simply enjoys sharing your thoughts with the collective consciousness of the blogosphere, and this is your purpose for blogging...well, this article is NOT for you. If however, you are someone who wants and NEEDS to make more money and you want to blog to do it, read on as I'll share two of my top tips.

Do it with Data Feeds!

Simply stated, you pick a vertical niche, several vendors who market in this niche, and make your blog a compendium of original content, news feeds, etc as usual...BUT, you also pull the RSS feed for a catalog that offers lots of products that serve this market. Most of the vendors in the major markets open their feed up to your affiliate clearinghouse (CJ, Linkshare, et al) and you are going to apply for the program, and then request the feed. Wordpress will do this for you phenomenally well. You need a FEW plugins and a couple of minor tweaks and you are OFF to the races in rapid-fire turnaround time, easy money on autopilot. (Especially because you can future date the posts for weeks, months and even years to come..;-)

The fortune really IS in the list

If you aren't yet ready for creating an avalanche of affiliate sales through data feeds, why not start offering some products visa VI your opt-in sequence? It always amazes me how few "bloggers" are incorporating direct response marketing into the mix - they will prominently display their feed count numbers, but most don't have a REAL email sign up from anywhere in sight. How many blogs have YOU visited once...loved the content, and simply forgot about over time as real-life intervened? (Or newer blogs occupied your mind space) I know I have forgotten about FAR more good ones than I can even remember...but a lot of MEDIOCRE ones I visit regularly. Why? It's quite simple. They email me offers. I signed up once...and they keep the party going by staying in touch.

CHAPTER SEVEN

AUTOPILOT MONEY MAKING WEBSITES

What is the purpose of your website? Have you ever asked yourself this question? If you want to make money online, then you will need to build autopilot money making a website that works with or without you. This is the best thing about making money online, automation. Because of automation, you can spend your time having a vacation while your website doing all the selling and making money for you.

If you are looking for ways to make autopilot money, then you must start with your website. If you already have a website, that will be even greater. Back to the question, what is the main reason for your website? The only answer is this, to sell something and to make money. I bet that you don't have to spend 2 months just to come up with a nicely designed website that impresses visitors, but can't make any money, right?

Therefore, the first thing you have to learn is to build an autopilot money making website. Remember, your website has only one main focus, which will be to make sales. Having tons of links only will make your visitors confused. You have to build your website in such a way that it directs visitors to do what you told them to do.

And in most cases, when visitors reach your autopilot money making website, they only have two choices. The first choice is that they buy your products there. And the second choice is this; leave their email and other contact information. The first option is not a good one because almost everyone will not buy something the first time they arrive at your website, this is common sense.

The better approach will be the second option, they come to your website, and they leave their email and contact information there. Usually, we called this kind of website a lead capture page or a squeeze page. The main purpose you capture their emails and contact information is because you can follow up with them, using emails. The tricks you can use to attract people to leave their contact with you are by giving away freebies like an e-book or a report.

This trick works wonder because people come to your website to look for the information that they want, and if you can provide them for free, they will just subscribe to it. After they have signed up in your autopilot money making a website, you can then send follow up emails to them using an autoresponder. This is how the sales are made, not from websites, but through emails.

So you can see now, the best way to create an autopilot income is by building autopilot money making a website that works for you 24 hours even while you sleep. All of the top gurus out there have their own lead capture page and their very own list of subscribers, so why don't you start to build your own today?

Websites That Makes You Money

Can you imagine earning a steady income online without having to do any extra work? If you want financial freedom faster, you need to get acquainted with autopilot money making websites. From that word "autopilot," it simply suggests that it's totally hands-free. The next generation of making money online which some smart people are already taking advantage of is residual income.

Residual income is possible on the internet. It's passive; you literally do the work once and then relax and enjoy the constant flow of cash to your bank account. Are you getting a hold of this? Well, some online business pays you a one-time commission when you make a sale for them. Others will reward you for life as long as the customer you refer to still retains her membership.

Autopilot money making websites are websites that allow you to affiliate with them for free; they are usually membership sites that have a fee for usage. Services like autoresponder, web hosting, domain registration, dating sites are good examples.

When you sign up to promote their services to the target market, you will earn a residual income for years to come, provided your referral keeps renewing her membership to the site. As easy as this business can be, so many people have failed because they embarked on it half prepared. You should be ready to put in the work required to set the income in motion. This is something you just have to do once, but reap the reward for life. The autopilot income is possible but you need to first automate it.

There are so many autopilot money making websites out there. What you should look for is the one that matches your preferences. What is your niche, do you like dating or you feel more comfortable with internet marketing? Whatever you have passion for is what will earn you more money. Never promote any product you don't have a liking for, you are sure going to lose morale within a short time if you don't like what you are doing. I have a passion for internet marketing and that is why I stick with promoting affiliate programs under IM niche.

Generating targeted traffic to your autopilot money making websites is a great skill you need to master. Website traffic is the lifeblood of every online business, without it, failure is around the corner. You need to learn the tenets of driving the right kind of traffic to these membership sites. Article marketing still remains the best traffic generation system for any website. There are other methods though, find out the best for you and stick with it.

CHAPTER EIGHT

AUTOPILOT ARTICLE MARKETING

Lots have been said about article marketing in internet marketing circles. There are many mentors who have been able to sell millions of dollars' worth of e-books on how to do article marketing. Mentors aren't the only ones making money. Web scriptwriters are making money off of promoting software which creates directories for articles.

But does article marketing work?

The answer to that question varies, depending on who you ask.

But here's my opinion

Let me begin by telling you that I started article marketing six months ago. In that short amount of time, I have written numerous articles and have been featured in as many as 70 different directories. And though some of these directories, I've received RSS feeds, which allows my articles to get onto many other websites.

Some of my article titles have received as many as 10,000 results in a search engine directory.

Several of my websites have zoomed to the number one position in various top search engines. Although I have done other things to acquire a higher ranking in search engines, I feel that article marketing has done a majority of the work for me. But more than that, autopilot article marketing is the reason for my success with articles.

Here is how I implement autopilot article marketing

I start off by writing things that I know about. The first article I wrote was promoting a website about home organization. I discussed organizing your home, a topic that I was known was very popular, but wasn't too familiar with. Now that I am more familiar with this process, I write articles about things that tend to work for me and information that I "do" know about.

The question you may be asking yourself is, "how can I create an autopilot article marketing campaign?" Here's how. You need to just jump right in, and write about what you know.

Autopilot article marketing may be the ticket to helping your business get to the next level.

Title your Article the Right Way

Make it easier to keep track of the spread of your article on the internet by making sure that you create an article title that is not already in use. Just before I submit an article, I place quotes around the title of my article and plug it into google.com. If Google's search comes up with something, then I'll choose another title until my search comes up with "no results". If you do have an article title with "no results", you will be able to keep track of the sites that are hosting your article. After you have submitted the article, wait several days and do a search using the article title. Continue to do this every couple of days. If you submit between 10 to 15 different directories, you will be amazed by the results.

Write About What You Know

Write about something you know about. Make sure you have more knowledge on the topic than the average reader; otherwise, you'll probably want to change your topic. Give the readers something they don't already know. Do your research and write a unique article... it'll pay off in the long run.

Write-In a Conversational Manner

Write with comfort and ease. Keep it simple. Today's internet reader clicks ready, meaning if the article is tough to read, then they will click out of it and go on to the next article. Keep your tone friendly, but informative.

Keep Articles Short

Keep your articles short - between 500 to 750 words. Remember, your reader more than likely has a very short attention span. Give them the information quickly and in a direct manner. You'll have a greater chance of keeping your reader's attention, and getting them to click your links in your resource box.

Include a Resource Box

Be sure to include a link to your site at the end of each article every time. Not only will this help bring visitors to your squeeze page or sales offer, but it will also help build backlinks to your site.

Remember to give your readers a powerful call to action to get them to act immediately to your offer.

Re-Invest Your Profits

If you follow steps 1-5 above, you should soon see profits roll in. Now take a portion of those profits and buy articles. And continue to do so with the profits of those articles. This leaves you free to focus on other forms of marketing. By reinvesting your profits into articles, you create a never-ending income stream of more articles (which leads to profit in and of themselves) and profit to purchase more articles. This is the autopilot article marketing technique.

In my experience, autopilot article marketing has been (and continues to be) a fantastic income generator for me. To take advantage of autopilot article marketing yourself, make sure to write about what you know, with the right title, and in a conversational manner. Remember to keep your articles short and include a resource box with a call to action. Then, when you earn profits from your articles, re-invest it to create more articles, more traffic, and more income. Then, simply rinse and repeat.

Simple Tricks to Multiplying Your Traffic Almost Overnight

Do you want to get more mileage out of your article marketing system? Do you want more sales and more subscribers? Do you want to make more money by exploiting free traffic to the max? I'm sure the answer is yes! Well, continue reading to discover 3 simple tricks to multiply your traffic, almost overnight:

1. Focus on quantity. It's no big secret that the more articles you have out there, the more traffic you are going to get overall, all things being equal. Yet too many people focus on making their articles perfect and not having more articles out there. Having more articles all over the web translates to more backlinks, more exposure for your website and more chances to brand your business. There are two ways to increase quantity - spend more time churning out articles or hire a freelancer from Elance or Workaholics 4 Hire.

2. Churn out top-class information and improve the conversion rates of your resource boxes. Okay, that's 2 shortcuts. Seriously, though, it all translates to you getting more out of each article. You'll want to share information that is so good that readers have no choice but to click on your link and visit your website and see more of what you have.

3. Churn out articles on a regular basis. The truth is, more and more article writers are heading online and competition is only going to become fiercer. You need to crank out new articles regularly (less so after you have a bulk of articles driving traffic on autopilot for you) so that you keep your competitive marketing edge.

One of the most important things one can do when marketing on the Internet is to maintain patience. You have to be focused to see success online. When you have only a few subscribers or a few articles out there, you need to keep the big picture in mind. It is very hard to quantify anything with only a few articles or a few dozen subscribers. As a general rule, you need to have at least 100 articles out there on the Internet before you make any judgments.

If you only have 10 articles out there, you are not going to see as much traffic as someone who has 1000 articles submitted to the same directory. Sure, there will be a few articles that perform outstandingly for you, but even so, it's very hard to beat quantity.

Think in terms of quality and quantity when it comes to article marketing and you can't go wrong. If you're getting traffic from 10 articles, all you need to do is do 10 times what you're doing and get 100 articles out there and you will see an increase in traffic. That's why it is important you maintain patience because as every month goes by, you're adding more articles to the system and your traffic will therefore increase. And this will eventually turn out to be an automated traffic source for years to come. It is literally hands-free traffic. That is the awesome thing about doing article marketing for a long time. When you have a mass of articles out there, you can stop doing the work and you will still get traffic on autopilot.

Who else wants to talk about article marketing ideas? If you are trying to make real money from home WITHOUT a big budget, I simply can't think of a better way to do it that creating copious amounts of content and distributing it around the net in the form of an avalanche of articles. But unfortunately, like LOTS of things in life, sometimes that's simply NOT enough. What you COULD do, however, to ramp UP the effort is infinite and ONLY limited by your imagination. Let's look at 3 of my favorites.

Using Articles In Your Data Feed Sites

If you aren't using data feeds sites to make money, you are leaving LOTS of it on the table. You can combine the power of your own original articles, with data feed products, and turn a simple Wordpress blog into an autopilot money maker quicker than it takes to make a ham sandwich for lunch.

Using articles For Remote Blogs

Do you Squidoo, hop around hub pages or even surf the wild and woolly world of Word press blogs that are NOT the self-hosted variety? This is a dead-simple way to repurpose your article content in imaginative new ways as part and parcel of a feeder/money site network that builds BIG backlinks (and bucks) in a hurry if you know what you're doing.

How About Articles for Pay Per Click Marketing Magic?

I love doing this and ALWAYS wonder why more people don't. Worried about the Google slap? Worry no longer, my dear friend. Simply "slapback" by putting your articles up on your landing page with calls to action weaved in within each paragraph - or even link OUT to your articles from a site map at the bottom of your landing page. So easy to do, and avoids the deleterious demons of a quality score that is lower than the Oakland Raiders win count so far in the season. (And if you aren't a football fan - that isn't high).

CONCLUSION

In conclusion, there are a few things you have to be mentally prepared when you make money online. When you are building your website, it's very easy to get stuck in the JOB mentality of "when I do work, I want to get paid". It can be discouraging to work 6 hours on an article, then not see money coming in. After a few weeks or months of it not making money, it feels even worse, like you wasted your time.

A few affiliate marketers who followed my email course came back and dropped me the same feedback saying that their blogs are not working and not making any money. I'm no stranger to those feelings. I had the same experience when I first started.

www.ingramcontent.com/pod-product-compliance
Lightning Source LLC
Chambersburg PA
CBHW070425220526
45466CB00004B/1552